Peace

AND

Joy

GUIDEBOOK

YOUR PATH TO
EMBRACING LIFE

CLANCY KIENER, LMFT

Peace & Joy Guidebook: Your Path to Embracing Life
Published by Quiet Mind Enterprises
Nashville, Tennessee

ISBN: 979-8-218-05132-7
SELF-HELP / Personal Growth / Happiness

Cover and Interior design by Victoria Wolf, wolfdesignandmarketing.com, copyright owned by Clancy Kiener.

This book is dedicated to my beautiful daughter, Sarah Carroll. You are more amazing than you will ever know! I love you!

Preface:

THE WHY OF IT

"Speech is power: speech is to
persuade, to convert, to compel."

—Ralph Waldo Emerson

When I reflect on why I wanted to write this book, I immediately relate it to my preaching. For many years, I didn't think I could preach, although I aspired to, and I often had ideas about what I wanted to convey in my sermons if I could. I always was and still am a quiet person.

When I was growing up, I never wanted to stand out or be noticed. When I was in the sixth grade, the teacher offered a way to earn extra credit by telling the class about a story that was in the news. I couldn't figure out why more students didn't take advantage of this. I watched the news most evenings, so one day I let the teacher know I was ready to tell a story from the news. But when I began talking and everyone looked at me, I became so self-conscious that I stopped midway and declined to say anything else. I never finished the story.

As I got older, I had less fear of public speaking, but I've always remained an introvert. I tend to draw some energy from other people but gain more from introspection. Then one day, I learned that I could use my introspection to develop sermons. I was able to look inside myself and identify with scripture on a level that resonated with others.

Thanks to my start with a small church in Tennessee, I became a preacher. My husband and I attended this church for about fifteen years. When the minister was away, a layperson would lead the worship service. One such person, whom I will call Matthew, changed my life. As I listened to Matthew, I was awestruck. He was in front of the whole congregation and spoke with a level of humility I immensely admired. When speaking of the beheading of John the Baptist, he admitted that he did not know how to interpret that act. At that moment, I thought that if he could get up there and be honest about not knowing what to say, I could certainly speak to the congregation too. I realized we don't have to know all the answers to offer helpful ideas and advice. Since then, I have had the honor of speaking in churches and a variety of other venues.

The messages in my sermons often translate into my therapy, and vice versa. As a licensed marriage and family therapist, I have opportunities to share concepts from preaching and life lessons with my clients. After preaching for more than fifteen years and working in the mental health field for about the same period, I find many ideas that are valuable in both spheres. I am honored to share the messages throughout this book and hope they will resonate with clients and others who can read them at their leisure. May this book give you the opportunity to find peace and joy through the reflections I've gained while fulfilling my passions of preaching and working as a therapist.

Chapter 1.

FINDING COURAGE

"The hardest victory is over self."

—Aristotle

When I was about six years old, I thought I was going to die in paradise. Ironically, what I thought would kill me helped me live more freely. I remember every part of the event as if it were yesterday. About forty-five years ago, I lived on Anna Maria Island in Florida, a sweet spot of the world. The sand was incredibly white, and it felt like cotton on my feet. The water was a shade of blue I had never seen before. That blue could never be recreated by a human. It was as if God was showing off, saying, "Look at the beauty I created."

My mother and I lived in a studio apartment on the beach in a place called Sandy Toes Apartments. I enjoyed making sandcastles and sitting on the beach with my mother. She was uncommonly beautiful. At the time, she was in her midtwenties. Her skin was a deep brown, thanks to Coppertone. Her dark skin made her long, light-blond hair even more noticeable by contrast. She would lie on the beach, deepening her tan and smoking her cigarettes.

What I liked most about that time was playing in the ocean. Even back then, I felt the water held spirituality, which could not be put into words. Sometimes the heart just knows what the head cannot say. I would swim and swim and swim. I had no fear of the water whatsoever … until I almost died.

On this dreadful day in 1978, I was happy as a clam swimming in the water, with no care in the world, and then suddenly—*boom*! A wave slammed in and hit me from behind. I was pushed below the surface and struggled to hold my breath. I didn't think I would survive. I couldn't breathe, I couldn't control my movements, and the wave had me—I could do nothing to help myself. I remember thinking, *I am way too young to die*. I was only six years old! I felt a fear beyond any I had known. It was possibly the biggest fear of all—the fear of death! In a few moments, my feet found the sand and I was able to stand. I was so happy to touch the ocean floor; I was so happy to breathe. I felt like I had been in that wave struggling for an hour, though it was probably less than a minute. I ran out of the water, straight to my mom, and sat beside her. After that scary event, I became extremely careful about the ocean and only wanted to swim in calm water. I was scared of waves because I knew those waves could leave me powerless!

A couple of weeks later, I met a girl whom I quickly considered one of my best friends. (Everybody was my best friend unless I hated them, and I didn't really hate anybody, so she was my best friend.) She was visiting Florida from Michigan, as did many people who lived in northern states. She was my age, and she told me I was the nicest person she had ever met. I wanted her to keep liking me, so I gave her some of my favorite stickers with colorful images of dogs. I liked her and watched out for her, so I was upset when she decided to go out into the ocean on a day when the waves were bigger than I had ever seen them before. I was worried for my best friend's safety.

4

I had lived on the beach for a while, and she was a tourist, so I thought it was my job to protect her. I told her what I had learned from the big wave that almost took me down forever. I told her it was unsafe to go into the water when the waves were so big. On this day, the waves looked like blue monsters that were at least twenty feet tall. These were the kind of waves that fueled my nightmares. I told her about the danger, and I urged her not to go. I wondered where her mother was, who was watching her, and who would warn her about the danger besides me. But no one did, and she ignored my advice. She went deeper and deeper into the water, and I was terrified for her. I knew that if I were out there, I would not survive, so I didn't think she would survive either.

An amazing thing happened. She not only lived through the big blue wave monsters, but she was having fun—laughing, jumping, and playing. She was not getting hurt at all. As I thought about what was happening, I felt myself getting upset. I concluded that she must be a superhero, and I was sad that she hadn't told me that. How could she be my best friend and not tell me she was a superhero? I was not only jealous of her superhero status; I was jealous of her having fun and not telling me she was a superhero. As I thought more about this, I felt anger welling up. When she came out of the water smiling and laughing and energized, I tried to get her to tell me about her superpowers.

She had no idea what I was feeling. I remember asking her calmly, "How are you able to play in such big waves?" I couldn't tell her how I felt. As an adult, I can talk more about my feelings, but when I was younger, I just held them inside. She looked at me and said with a kind and happy tone in her voice, "I go under the wave." That made me even more angry. How could my best friend lie to me? Why wouldn't she tell me about her superhero powers? But I still didn't tell her how I felt.

I watched her have fun for a little while longer while I sat on the shore. As I sat there, I realized that the true feeling under my anger was fear. I did not want to risk going into the same situation that had almost killed me. I was uncertain if I could survive it. But I didn't want to stay on the sidelines and just watch from the beach. Deep down, I wanted to trust what my friend said, that she simply went under the waves. I decided to fight through the fear, find my reserve of courage, and have faith in my friend.

I was scared, but I quickly swam over beside my friend. She said, "Here comes a wave." I looked up at what appeared to be a twenty-five-foot wall of water coming at me, though it was most likely much smaller. All I could see was this massive wall. **This was the biggest wave I had ever seen!** I looked over at my friend and hoped she was telling me the truth. I saw her dive under this wave about five seconds before it hit, and I did the same. I was going into the belly of the beast. This was a leap of faith.

As I dove, I felt a slight pressure on my body, and I went deeper. Everything happened in slow motion. I could feel the water changing as the wave passed, creating a feeling of comfort.

As I looked down, an undertow made the sand move slowly, and the seaweed did a slow dance. Everything was quiet, and everything moved slowly. The warm water surrounded me, held me, and kept me safe as the wave broke above me. My mind was quiet, and everything was okay. I felt at peace. We both popped our heads above the surface, and my smile was as big as hers. I would like to thank my friend for helping me take this leap of faith, for helping me find the courage to face my fears, and for helping me find peace under the water. I was right—she's a superhero!

As an adult, at times, I have felt an abundance of emotions that overwhelm me. I have seen people seeming to have fun while I am tossed in a wave of emotion. I have joined others having fun and tried to look like I was, too, when actually my emotions were coming at me like a twenty-five-foot wave. I realize now that I was judging my insides based on other people's outsides. Often, people do not share their emotions, so it seemed that other people did not have as much fear, worry, or other emotions as I had. Through my attendance at twelve-step meetings and my work as a counselor, I have learned that everyone has been in a wave of emotion. While we are being thrashed about in a wave, it can be almost impossible to ask for help. For some who are in a wave, it can be difficult to trust in a Higher Power, and it can be overwhelming to try to wait it out. They can lose control and find it hard to breathe. The wave can leave us powerless, and life can feel unmanageable.

As a grownup living in a grownup world, I have witnessed the wave as addiction, isolation, and issues from the past coming up to meet us again. The wave can also be shame, rage, fear, or depression. No two waves are alike, but many are similar, and often our feelings about them are also similar. It can feel like we will never escape. We start to search for a way out, sometimes any way out. For some, addiction seems like a way out—using to mask our real feelings. This can create a bigger wave. Masking our true feelings, our true selves, may seem like a good option. We hide our feelings because we don't want to go further into the wave, but this choice, too, is counterintuitive as it keeps us away from the people who can help us learn how to go under the wave. We hide behind our monetary success, our looks, or our significant other. We can lose ourselves, and the wave can turn our world upside down.

In this upside-down world, we can hide who we are because we don't want people to see us as we are. We can feel ashamed. We can become dishonest, and our lives can feel darker. Others can feel it's not appropriate to ask questions and really get to know us, and we can be scared to let others in. We can be scared to know ourselves. We can show the world only a small version of ourselves, not really letting people know who we are. We can pretend to be someone else, someone who is okay. When we don't find the courage to live honestly, we don't allow others to know who we are, and we may forget who we are. We may turn against ourselves, trying to dismiss the vulnerable part of ourselves, the sadness, the fear, and the neediness. We may ignore a part of ourselves so we can breathe, and we may become so resentful toward that vulnerable part of ourselves that we turn against it. We can lose a beautiful, emotional, sensitive part of ourselves that is attuned to the connection with God.

When we resist being in the wave and feel powerless, it can make life seem unmanageable. We often need to admit our powerlessness to be free. When we do, God will enable a journey within us to gain the power of introspection. It is in this place—the place that is open, light, and honest—that we meet God and find the courage to connect with others. This is the place of love.

God is there for us. Sometimes we just need to look at ourselves to see God. When we turn against ourselves, it can become harder to feel that connection with God. God is in the sadness, the sensitivity, and the vulnerable. God is most definitely under the wave! God helps bring us to the peace that is under the wave. God helps bring us to us.

I was talking with a friend recently about a deeper level of powerlessness. Through these conversations, I gained more knowledge about what is under the wave. When we have the honesty and self-awareness to admit that we are powerless over so much in life—such as addiction, love, and passion—then we are freer to live our lives without the burden of trying to be in control of the wave. We can work with each other and with God to change what we can and release what we cannot change. Ultimately, we cannot change others, but we have an impact on others, and they on us, when we let them.

My friend from the beach did not listen to me when I told her she could be hurt or killed in the wave. I saw her having fun, and then I followed her. My warnings had no impact on my friend, but her courage had an impact on me. As a society, we tend to forget the impact we can have on others.

One theory about the origin of the serenity prayer points to the German Pietist Friedrich Oetinger, who, in the eighteenth century, wrote the words, "God give me the detachment to accept those things I cannot alter, the courage to alter those things I can alter, and the wisdom to distinguish the one thing from the other."

I have my own version of a prayer that helps me determine what I should take on and what I need to leave alone: "God help my thoughts be your thoughts through me, help my words be your words through me, and help my actions be your actions through me."

I can alter many situations that could end up doing harm. If my friend had listened to me about the wave, she would have been waiting on the shore with me. I needed to respect her enough to allow her to make her choice, and in turn, I learned from her choice.

Sometimes, it's difficult to summon the courage we need to keep moving forward in life. I fall short, and other people fall short. We are human. Whether at church, in a twelve-step program, or just by living life on life's terms, isn't love the ideal? My hope for you is that you have the courage to open your heart and allow love in. After all, it is through love that we become closer to ourselves, to God, and to each other. It is here in this place, the place of understanding our connection with love, that the upside-down world becomes right-side up! It is underneath all the BS of the world—the struggles, the chaos, and the waves—that we find the connection, the love! When we allow love in, when we let go and allow God to do the work, the world becomes brighter.

A place within my heart is the connection to my spirituality. God meets us where we are. God meets us when we are hurting, scared, disconnected, and damaged. God will lead us to love and light if we allow it. I have seen this power in the helpers, the healers, and the empathizers.

All it takes is a mustard seed of faith. Faith is the courage to live through the fear. We can look inside ourselves, under the BS, under the wave, to find the ultimate peace, which is love. I urge you to find the courage to allow yourself to go under the wave and open your heart to love.

Chapter 2.

QUIETING OUR MINDS

"Learn to be silent. Let your quiet mind listen and absorb."

—Pythagoras

When my Grandmother turned seventy-five, my mother and I decided to drive from Nashville to Champaign, Illinois, for her birthday party. I thought since we were going that way, we should stop in Chicago. We did not make any specific plans for this trip; we decided to just wing it.

If I can monitor where I am, I tend to feel okay in unfamiliar places. I heard once that birds have a focal point when flying, a place they can easily see to gain perspective and determine their location. I have found that to be helpful when I am traveling. When my mother and I went to Chicago, I decided I would use the Willis Tower, known to me at the time as the Sears Tower, as my focal point.

A few hours after we left Nashville, we made it to our hotel. From there, I looked for the Sears Tower. I could not see it, but I was determined that after we had a chance to relax in our room, it would appear when we went back out. We ordered coffee, which took about an hour and a half and cost twenty-five dollars, and then we went outside to explore. The second we were outside the hotel, I noticed a constant hum of people and cars. There was far more activity than I was used to in Nashville. Part of me was excited, and part of me was anxious because we did not know where we were going. We roamed around the city for a couple of hours, and I still didn't see the tower. Its absence made me more anxious.

One of our first stops was the zoo. Hundreds of children were there—so many that I couldn't see the ground. All I could see was an endless sea of little heads. The zoo was a jumble of lines, people, children, and noise. Outside the zoo, I saw malls and stores and restaurants … and people and more people.

It seemed Chicago had everything except the Sears Tower. I couldn't find my focal point. I asked my mother where the tower was, and she said she didn't know. I didn't want to ask the taxi driver because I wanted him to focus on driving. I found myself getting more and more anxious … the taxis, the people, the lines, the noise. I looked for the Sears Tower while we rode in the taxi and while we walked, but it was nowhere in sight. Where could it be?

We went back to the hotel room, had coffee—again—had dinner, and slept. The next day, we were heading to Champaign, so we made sure we had our bags packed the night before. We were glad to be leaving. The hotel was nice, but we were charged for everything, and the employees seemed tired. I found myself with the kind of anxiety that puts pressure on my chest and gives me a slight feeling of fight or flight.

The next day, I woke up at 4:00 a.m. I woke up my mom, and we were out of that room in no time. I told my mom I would wait outside with our bags while she checked out. I went outside, and there were no people, no cars, and no noises. Everything was quiet. I found myself breathing slower, and my muscles relaxed. I took a deep breath and looked across the street and up at the sky, and there it was! The Sears Tower! It was right across the street from the hotel. It was right there all along. I couldn't see it before because I was stressed. I couldn't see it because of the noise. I couldn't see it because I was looking at everything else and did not look at what was right in front of me. I couldn't see it because I didn't look up.

To look up, I needed to stop focusing on the chaos of the city and quiet my mind so I could see my focal point—that stable landmark that would help me find my way. I had to lose the noise first.

Some of us face a different kind of challenge when we become too comfortable with the noise of our lives. We become so accustomed to chaos that we do not even know it is there. We worry about what will happen if we lose the noise. After all, it is what we know; it has often become an integral part of us … of who we are. It takes courage to reject the familiar noise and chaos of our lives and embrace a quieter existence so we can find our true path.

When I was getting clean and sober, I had an ever-present hustle and bustle of activity in my head. One constant element of this noise was a desire to drink. I was scared to lose that desire because drinking was my relief, but quitting drinking came with even more noise. It came with jealousy that others could drink and I could not. It came with sadness for the loss. I didn't know what could replace these feelings, and I was scared to lose them. I became so accustomed to that desire that it was just an extension of me. I didn't drink exceptionally long in my life, but I did feel I needed it. I felt I needed it to quiet the noise.

People use many ways to quiet the noise in their minds, including sex, co-dependency, and money. For me, it was alcohol.

One day while I was actively in recovery, I saw some people I knew from my days of drinking. I felt I needed to join them, but then I didn't want to join them. I felt like I was having an out-of-body experience. I picked up the telephone to try to get support and find someone to talk me out of drinking. After calling people who either did not care or did not answer their phones, I looked up and with my whole self, everything in me, I said, "Help." It was not a scream but a whisper … "Help." But the emotion behind it was crying out so loud to God that the sound could have shaken the heavens. It was a plea. I begged God with everything I had in this whisper.

Suddenly, I lost all the noise and it was replaced with faith in God. I felt the desire, the obsession, and the need to drink leave. It never came back. I was free. I had asked for help with everything I had in me, and God answered. God waited until I was willing to give up the addiction. God waited for me to look up. God doesn't take what we're not willing to give. God does not force us to look up. I didn't know how strong this desire to drink was until it went away. I didn't know what it would be replaced with until I found it was replaced with a feeling that I would be okay, I had hope, and I had more faith than before I asked for help. God not only helped me find some semblance of sanity but also freedom from the bondage of self, the bondage of addiction. God helped me quiet my mind and open my heart to find my focal point … God.

Often, we yearn for a feeling that is so close, but we can't seem to reach it. We know that a feeling of calm, quiet, and peace is right there, but it can still feel elusive. We can be afraid to give up the busyness of our lives that we're more familiar with and replace it with a better option. We can be afraid of connecting with ourselves and God. When we yearn to connect our head, heart, and spirit, we realize that the goal that seemed so distant is closer than we thought. It is difficult to make this connection alone. God assists in that journey when we allow it.

I went to AA meetings and to therapy, and I talked to friends and a sponsor. I did all the physical and emotional work I could with others. It was then time for me to meet God by myself. It was a leap of faith. It is in this place where I have seen others cast off what addiction, anger, fear, and the rest of the noise have caused them to become and find who they are with a quiet mind. I have seen hardened people become poets, I have seen angry people cry, and I have seen trust in a God that enables vulnerability. I have seen the upside-down world turn right-side up.

At times, we work together to bring each other to a focal point—to love—and at times we work alone as we come to understand our own metaphysical connection to God. For many, it is in that alone space that they can understand the light within. In that solitude, we can better understand our light and, with that understanding, see the light in others—the love. After all, isn't love about seeing the light in others even if they do not see the light in us? Sometimes we can bring each other to the desire and the passion for awareness, but often, it happens only in that place of solitude, the meeting between God and me, and you and God. In that place, we can understand the connection to the light, the ever-shining light. God not only returns us to sanity but also illuminates the light for all to see. When I stopped drinking and became connected with God, myself, and that quiet place within, I started to discover who I really am. Perhaps seeing the light, removing the noise, and taking a leap of faith help us be who we really are: children of our Creator.

Chapter 3.

LETTING GO OF HARMFUL FEELINGS

"Cast all your anxiety on him because
he cares for you."

—1 Peter 5:7
(New International Version)

God will not take anything we do not give to God. If we want to keep our addiction, our anger, or our resentment—whatever it is we're holding onto—and we're not ready to give it over to God, we can keep it. God can help make us ready, but even with that, we must allow God. God will meet us where we are.

Once we have come to this place of understanding that God can restore us to sanity and our life will be better for it, we are at the place where we are ready, willing, and able to let go of the issues that are our albatrosses. Doing this gives us the freedom to live life on life's terms, to stop wanting to control everybody and everything, and to let it go. It is then that we are more aware of other people, ourselves, and God.

I am a licensed marriage and family therapist who used to specialize in working with people who have issues of addiction. I now specialize in working with people who get in their own way of success. For some, success is measured in a passion—for wealth, leadership, or fame—and for others, success is about finding balance. There is a common formula I have seen for most people who attain success. I have found that the root of success comes from knowing oneself, others, and a Higher Power (whatever form that may take) and allowing the self to be the self without getting in its own way. God can help us know ourselves and others.

God shows God's essence through people. When our hearts are open, God is able, through others, to help us understand others, ourselves, and God. We might receive this understanding at a church, and often the minister's message feels like it's just for us. We could receive this understanding while others are talking around us, and we hear exactly what we need to hear at the time. We could also receive it at a concert through a song that moves our soul. Bob Dylan's "Make You Feel My Love" does that to me. This experience could be at a museum, seeing a painting so cathartic that it seems like looking at proof of God's existence. We can receive this gift of understanding at a self-help meeting from someone who is struggling, and we then know we are not the only one. God meets us where we are! Perhaps, then, it is better to know where we are without denying it.

There have been times when I felt alone in sadness or darkness and I thought I was wrong for feeling that way. Through divine guidance, education, experiences, and other people, I've learned that feelings themselves are just fine; they are not wrong. At times, we see what we don't like about ourselves, what we perceive as wrong, and then we realize that we are just fine as we are. Getting to the root of our value as a person is how we learn to live as if we are not sleeping. It's how we wake up. The old self then becomes the new self, or the self that was always there but not always seen. We discover the part of our consciousness that has been present the whole time, the part that has always been awake, and the part that we buried under self-doubt, anger, or fear. When we allow ourselves to feel those feelings and not fight them, they often relinquish their power. God helps us with that. God enables us to go through those feelings, and God will take away the burden we feel once we have processed through them.

I don't tell clients to turn over their feelings to a Higher Power before they are ready. When they are ready, they often know to do it without me suggesting it. Gaining an understanding of their own feelings can assist with them being ready. For instance, if clients come into my office and want to be able to forgive those who hurt them, it is often necessary to look at the reasons why the forgiveness is stagnating. If clients come into my office and want their anger to leave, it is necessary to look at the reason they are angry. If clients come into my office and want to be more connected with people, it is helpful to look at the reason they are not. Often, the reason they're stuck is that they're trying to protect themselves. It would be great if telling clients they should not be angry would fix the situation.

I have worked with people who have been abused and haven't been able to voice how they feel until they come into my office. I have no right to tell them not to be angry about the abuse, and when I hear their stories, I'm angry too. I have heard stories from people who were bullied when they were young, and as adults, they have difficulty connecting with people. Of course they do! People feel how they feel for a reason. My clients and I explore how anger is a defense against letting people in. Not being social, being detached, and disassociating are defenses against being hurt again. Everybody has a right to such defenses, but often the defenses are tools that worked at one time and are no longer necessary.

Part of the issue may lie not in feeling the way we do but in believing it's not okay to feel the way we do. When we fight our feelings, we often end up on top of the wave and find that we're fighting against ourselves. When we stop fighting against ourselves and our feelings, we can go deeper and identify the root of our feelings. Once we find and process the root, we can often let go of unwanted feelings.

In looking at my feelings and becoming ready to let them go and turn them over to God, I find it is helpful to name the feeling, allow myself to feel it, determine where it came from, and realize that having the feeling does not make me a bad person. Having a feeling makes me a person who feels. We need to understand what gave rise to a challenging feeling in order to be ready to release it.

When I was around four to five years old, I lived in Illinois. In the winter, it snowed so much that the snow would create a slide from the top of our dog shed to the ground. The dog shed was about ten feet tall. I would go to the top of the shed and slide to the bottom. Then one day, when I was at the top and getting ready to slide down, I saw several dogs at the bottom. I was afraid of them, so I stayed on top of this snow slide for as long as I could until my toes got too cold to bear. I slowly got down and ran inside to warm up my toes.

A couple of months later, my stepdad saw my mom's car

buried in snow and decided we should move to Orlando to be with his family in warmer climes. In Orlando, I had many opportunities to play on water slides. But I found that I was afraid of water slides and all other slides. Years later, I was trying to figure out what I was feeling that kept me from enjoying the slides. The feeling was fear. I felt unsafe, not knowing what would happen when I got to the bottom and being fearful of getting stuck at the top. I allowed myself to feel that fear.

I investigated with kindness where the root of that fear began, and I remembered more clearly the fear I had when I felt threatened by the dogs at the bottom of the dog shed. I had been so scared when I thought I couldn't come down. I gave myself permission to feel that fear without judging myself for feeling it. I then realized that I had my fear, but my fear didn't have me. Once I better understood how I acquired that fear, I was able to let go of the situation that generated it, and it no longer had any effect on me. I fully understood that the trauma of being on that snow slide translated into my fear of the water slides. The real issue was not with the water slides but with the fear that the snow slide produced.

For some, processing feelings may not be as simple as my experience. The slide could represent physical or verbal abuse, the dogs could be anger from a family member, and the snow could be cold treatment from others. Feelings are not always as easy to process as my fear of slides. However, looking at the root of a feeling, examining what caused it and how we are affected by it, and knowing that feeling is okay can help us let it go. Sometimes we do this alone; sometimes we have help from others.

What is on the other side of letting go of emotions that we once held onto as tools for survival? Vulnerability and taking the risk of being hurt by opening our hearts are on the other side. The good news is that we can be vulnerable with a trusted person, with ourselves, and with God. That level of honesty can be our focal point and our stronghold to knowing ourselves, others, and God. When we know ourselves, we become less vulnerable to the harms our world can deliver. That doesn't mean we will never feel sad, angry, or negative, but we will be less impacted by our past. God wants us to experience this freedom from the bondage of ourselves. God wants the albatross of our pain to leave us. Sometimes this happens through others, and sometimes we are brought by others to a place where we can allow the pain to leave in solitude.

But then what? What do we do when we are free from the bondage of our own negative thoughts and challenging feelings? We learn that sometimes it is our job to be helped, and sometimes it is our job to help. How do we know which is which? How do we know the path God wishes for us to take in order to release us from the bondage of self? It is a journey, not a destination.

Does God have a path in mind for us, and if so, how do we find it? How does free will play into our journey to match God's will with our own? Some of us may have longed to know that path, God's path. My belief is that God's will does not impose only one path.

I once worked at a furniture store in Brentwood, Tennessee. I loved the work, and I loved the people I worked with. In addition to working with an amazing manager, I loved the customers. I met some of the kindest people I have ever known. I'm glad for the experience, and I'm even more grateful than I would have realized at the time for the education I received. You can really get to know people when selling them furniture.

One of the best educational experiences came from a large family that stopped by on a Sunday. They were gentle, kind, and very religious. They wanted a couch and were not sure of the best one for them. They had a process: they tried the couches, discussed the purchase, and, if they all agreed it could be the best fit, they prayed about it. After looking for a while and talking about the options, they found a couch they agreed could be the best fit, so they went out to the parking lot. I asked the salesperson what they were doing, and he said, "Praying about the couch." They apparently received the message that it was the correct purchase for them, and they bought the couch.

Perhaps it was not the one and only couch for them. A loving God does not have only one path for us. God is powerful enough to meet us where we are and work with us, through us, and for us. If we choose a path of love and kindness, if we do our best to do no harm, then we may see many paths to choose from.

If we choose a path that hurts us or others, we get in our own way. We collect more baggage, and we tend to keep that stuff with us until we let go of it or it changes us. What about decisions that are bigger than buying a couch? What about when we make the wrong choice on an important matter, and we know it? It is in that place that God works for us even more than we can imagine. God can even turn a destructive path into one that is constructive. God meets us where we are!

We have an innate desire to create the best life for ourselves. We gather protection in order to live our lives the best we can. This protection comes in the form of beliefs, feelings, and character traits that may have been useful once but later in life can hold us back. Just as hoarders hold onto their stuff, we internally hold onto beliefs and behaviors we believe will enable us to have the best life possible. Often this protects us from harm. But there may come a day when we discover we do not need that protection any longer. When that happens, we can take an inventory of our feelings, beliefs, and characteristics. We can enable ourselves to further understand what we don't need and what holds us back from living fully. When we understand what we would like to give up, asking for help is often the best and quickest path to letting go of our challenges. Talking the situation through, looking at it from a different angle, and asking a Higher Power to take it often allows us to let that stuff go!

Chapter 4.

LIVING FULLY
ALIVE

"It is not the length of life, but the depth of life."

—Ralph Waldo Emerson

When I work with people who have physical illnesses that make them unable to leave their homes for long, if at all, I find that they often feel regret for the life they did not fully live when they were healthy. I often hear them say that if they knew then, when they were physically healthy, what they know now, they would have lived a fuller life. I feel that people who are physically healthy but who don't live with passion and vigor as if they are awake have little advantage over those who are losing their health. I have had clients in dire situations who search to live life more fully ... and then wake up. I have talked with people in jail, figuratively and literally, who search to find meaning in their lives. It seems some people have an innate desire to live fully alive. But what happens when that desire is not there? What happens when we are sleepwalking through our lives? It's helpful to look at the reasons why.

In the first chapter of this book, we learned it could be beneficial to have the courage to go under the wave, where we can find peace. The second chapter described achieving a quiet mind so we can find and follow our focal point. In the third chapter, we learned to identify feelings that are keeping us stuck and turn them over to God so we can create our path to a life of love and kindness. These steps lead us to a place where we can further understand what it means to relinquish feelings and beliefs that are holding us back.

In this chapter, we will look more specifically at how to move forward, as we now understand that we have been powerless over certain aspects of our lives, God has all power, and we can trust God. God wants us to be free of the bondage of self so we can fully live. It is by trusting whatever Higher Power we believe in that we can summon the courage to determine what is impeding our ability to live life in a state of passion, freedom, and joy. So the question becomes: What are you holding onto that you don't need anymore?

In my personal life and my professional life, I have known hoarders. Hoarding is a remarkably interesting phenomenon. Often, hoarders feel as if they are not in control of their lives, so they work hard to be in control of their things. This causes them to live an illusion. Hoarders are not in control of their things; they fall victim to their things. If you have seen the homes of hoarders, you have seen that their things control them.

How does someone become a hoarder? Behaviors like this do not happen in a vacuum, and often there are prior circumstances leading up to hoarding. Hoarders may start feeling like they are not in control of their lives and then a big event happens, solidifying that feeling. Their tool for coping with the feeling of not being in control is to try to control their space by holding onto their belongings. This may not be true of all hoarders, and only those experiencing this lifestyle can understand their own nuances. I have not walked in hoarders' shoes, so I cannot truly understand all the events that led them to create their situations. I can only know what I have researched, seen, and heard.

True hoarding can be triggered by an event that turns messiness into hoarding. A significant other may have left, a family member may have passed away, or a job may not have gone the way a person hoped. Those who become hoarders often feel they cannot control events outside their immediate environment, so they hold onto controlling stuff in their homes.

Hoarders generally don't want others to remove any of their stuff because it is their stuff and it is within their control, even if their environment becomes unsanitary and unsafe. They will declare it as their house, their stuff, and under their control. In some ways, this feeling of control makes them feel safe. People often wonder why hoarders keep the things they do, including items they no longer need.

Of course, we all do that to some extent. We may not hold onto unneeded physical possessions, but many of us hold onto defenses, character challenges, and other emotional impediments. Just as a hoarder may keep items they no longer need, we may keep traits that no longer serve us. And just as a hoarder can get comfortable with stuff that serves no purpose, we can become comfortable with characteristics that no longer serve us. These characteristics can become inherent to our understanding of who we are, and we may wonder what would happen if we no longer had them.

The standard term for these characteristics is character defects, but I call them character challenges. We are not defective, but we can embody characteristics as tools we once found helpful but that over the years have become challenges. If people live in an unsafe environment, they may acquire hypervigilance, a tool to keep them alive. Once out of the dangerous environment, they may not need that hypervigilance, yet even if it impedes their life, they may keep it because they perceive it as an essential part of their safety.

Periodically, it can be helpful to stop, look around, and take inventory of our lives and ourselves by asking what we are holding onto that we no longer need. What do we think we own that is, in fact, owning us? When we ask these questions, life has a way of providing answers.

About ten years ago, I met a man I'll call John. He was not a friend of mine but a friend of a friend; he traveled in my social circle. He was a good-looking older man who commanded a room, the kind of man people liked quickly. He always seemed happy and loved talking with others. He talked easily and comfortably. John was a nice person who never had anything bad to say. I could not understand why I did not like him.

I did not talk to many people about my feelings toward John, as he was in my social circle. The few people who did know how I felt could not understand my feelings either. I talked with a friend about my feelings, and I realized that the most notable trait John possessed was confidence. His confidence made people happy to talk with him and pleased to be in his presence. I agreed with my friend that John was a good person, but I still didn't like him. Although I understood that I did not have to like everybody, I wanted to figure out why I did not like John.

He had no impact on my life, I did not know him well at all, and I hardly ever saw him. But when I did, I was uncomfortable. I didn't want to be uncomfortable without knowing where the feeling was coming from, so I went to a quiet place and allowed myself to feel. As I allowed my mind to just flow where it wanted to go, I thought of William Shakespeare's quote, "The fault, dear Brutus, is not in our stars, but in ourselves, that we are underlings." That was it! John was so confident, and his confidence reminded me that in social situations, I was not confident. I felt like an underling.

Through this part of my journey of self-discovery, I understood that my feelings outweighed the situation. The issue was with me, not with John. When feelings outweigh a situation, the issue often is with the source of the feelings, not the situation. The reason I did not like John was not because he did anything wrong; it was because of my insecurities. I then worked on where this lack of confidence was coming from. I discovered that I had low social efficacy partially because for most of my life, I focused on others. To be confident in social situations, I would need to show people who I am. I wasn't sure who I was because I got lost while focusing on other people.

I found a mental health therapist, and I worked to understand myself more. I am now able to better understand myself, and I'm freer in social situations. I also understand that focusing primarily on others rather than on myself was a tool I needed while growing up. I no longer need that tool.

To lose that tool I once needed, I had to understand that

my reactions were sometimes out of proportion to actual situations. In the case of my dislike of John, I realized he was actually very kind. When I let go of that tool I had outgrown, I better understood who I was.

Most of us operate from a place where we can decide what we keep and what we give away. That may seem a simple concept, but it can get complicated. We don't always know what we don't need. This can create a vicious cycle. My insecurity bred jealousy, which bred animosity and then resentment. I resented how this man made me feel, but he made me feel the way he did because of my own jealousy. So, in fact, I made myself feel the way I felt.

We can hold onto anger, resentment, ego, and what we do not realize we no longer need. We can hold onto fear, shame, and anxiety, and often there is comfort in holding onto these feelings. They are our feelings, and we are comfortable with them.

Holding onto these harmful feelings and not acknowledging them can cause us harm. They can become a pathology. Like hoarders, we hold onto these negative feelings or traits until we can no longer find room for them. They start working their way outside of our house, outside of us, and what we thought we were keeping secret, other people start noticing. We try to close our doors and lock them so nobody can see, but eventually, we realize we are no longer able to hide our stuff. People start asking if we are okay. People start complaining about what they see because these feelings can invade others' environments.

When our stuff starts coming out in view, we may want to isolate ourselves. We may get laid off from a job, we may feel insecure in situations that are benign to others, and loved ones may become concerned about us. And we still do not know what to give up. Sometimes we even lose track of what we are holding onto. We can find the truth by going under the wave, by checking the ego. We can find our character challenges by trusting our focal point. We can find them by looking with honesty.

We may come to a point when we admit we are powerless over our character challenges and our stuff is making our lives unmanageable. Just as hoarders may realize they no longer have their stuff—their stuff has them—we may come to understand that we no longer have our character challenges—our character challenges have us.

There is hope.

What we can't do, God can. A power greater than us can help in this situation. When we realize we are not strong enough alone to clean up our house, God will meet us where we are if we allow it. God is stronger than us. God can help us manage our stuff.

It is obvious that hoarders cannot clean their houses by themselves. It is just too much, and they need help. Similarly, when we're trying to manage our character challenges, we may need a friend, therapist, spiritual mentor, family member, or another trusted individual to help. We must all work together to improve the areas we cannot fix alone. Once we admit that our house needs cleaning out, and we have even a mustard seed of faith that God will direct others to help, we will be able to find what to turn over and what to get rid of.

When we're turning over to God the feelings and beliefs that are holding us back, we can begin to understand the emotions behind our challenges. Through my conversation with my friend, I was able to recognize my character challenge of jealousy. I realized I had my jealousy, but my jealousy did not have me, and I conquered my negative feelings. I freed myself to live life more fully.

I did not say anything to John to let him know how I initially felt about him, but there are times in life when our feelings or character challenges do come out and affect another person negatively.

If I hurt others in some way and they let me know, I feel bad because I am human and I made a human mistake. But I do not feel I am bad. That is the difference between empathy and shame. We do not need other people to dictate our foundation of self. It is our job and our Higher Power's job to determine who we are. We all have a certain *je ne sais quoi* (a quality that cannot be described) that defines us.

No matter who we are, even if we have done bad things, we can be forgiven. That is grace. We do not earn grace; we are offered it as a gift. We know that a Higher Power forgives us, but we must also forgive ourselves. Perhaps at times, it is less about forgiving and more about reconciling.

We often develop characteristics that we use as tools to live our lives. As life goes on and we change, we may realize these tools are no longer helpful. To let go of the feelings and behaviors we no longer need, we may need to understand their source, talk with a trusted person, and release them to a Higher Power. It is not a simple or easy process, but it is one that allows us to live more fully!

Chapter 5.

MANAGING EMOTIONS ROOTED IN THE PAST

"You will not be punished for your anger;
you will be punished by your anger."

—Buddha

How do we reconcile past behaviors we regret? Sometimes it is best to write down memories of behaviors we regret, sometimes it is best to talk about them, and sometimes it is best to do both. We may look at where the behaviors came from and decide what emotions we want to give up. I have noticed that when I'm doing this, anger often comes to the surface. Anger can stem from other emotions, but what does our anger mean?

Anger is an interesting emotion. It can protect us, and sometimes we need it. It can feel safer to have our fists up than our arms out, and at times it is unsafe to have our arms out. Anger makes us feel powerful! It gives us big voices and makes us feel stronger than we are. We can intimidate others with our anger. We can get what we want, we can make people listen to us, and we do not have to be vulnerable. But we can get stuck in that behavior. We can name it as rage, hate, ego, or aggression. But it is anger, and it can mutate. We can forget it is with us, and it can come out at the strangest times. We can feel we do not have any control over it.

Anger often comes from fear, which is the reason we feel like we need our fists up rather than our arms out. This can be a fear of not being seen, heard, or understood. It can be a fear of not feeling important, loved, or cared for. Or a fear of being treated unfairly, losing something, or being hurt. Anger is good when it protects us from being hurt, but anger that stays inside can mutate. Once anger mutates, it can feel like an inherent part of ourselves, it can be strangely comforting, and we can feel that it defines who we are. This is false; we are not our anger. But what happens when we let it go? We may fear we will lose a part of ourselves, but letting go of anger can help us establish who we really are. When we let go of an emotion, the space we create must be replaced with something else. If we give up tools that are no longer working in our favor, they can be replaced with the light of our Creator. When anger leaves, that emptiness can be filled with love.

But what if we are angry at ourselves? Anger toward ourselves is debilitating. It grows out of beliefs that we are wrong or less than. These are false beliefs. If we hurt someone, our actions are wrong; who we are is not wrong. We are more than just our actions. If we wrong someone, we can make amends and move on. But if we feel that making that mistake means we are wrong as a person, we are saying that our Creator is wrong. God gives us grace. God loves us no matter what. If God can love us unconditionally, why can't we appreciate ourselves? Sometimes the answer goes back to our past.

What happens when a feeling is too big to unpack? The mind still tries, often in the form of looping thoughts, thoughts we can't seem to stop as we continue to examine an event over and over in different ways. We can get fixated on analyzing past events, with thoughts like *I can't believe he said that,* or *I can't believe that happened,* or *What was that about?* These looping thoughts can go on for years. When they do, it is often helpful to talk with someone to identify at what point the feeling became bigger than our ability to manage it.

When I was about seven years old, my friend and I were playing with seeds from a local tree. We put them in an upside-down horn on my bike. My friend accidentally knocked them down, and they scattered on the carport area of the trailer we were living in. My stepdad later asked me about them, and I said, "My friend did it." He did not believe me and said I was going to get a spanking for lying. I don't remember if I got the spanking, but I always remembered the fear I felt when he said that.

Through the years, I thought of this past event and was uncertain what to make of it. At times, the memory generated looping thoughts. I was thinking about this event more than I would have liked because I was trying to figure it out.

When I talked with someone about the enduring trauma of that experience, I was able to release the fear that I had been holding onto, and the looping thoughts went away. Turns out, the looping thoughts were about more than fear. I felt I had no control over what happened. I did something bad, and that meant I was bad, which made it a triggering event. When I was seven years old, my reaction was in proportion to the event. But I couldn't rectify my feelings over the years because they seemed out of proportion.

As an adult, due to a helpful conversation with a kind person, I realized I had done nothing wrong and I was simply a kid being a kid. The feeling of angst when I thought about this event went away, and I understood the situation more realistically. It was no longer bigger than me. My stepdad had been angry about seeds being spilled on the ground, and his reaction outweighed the situation. Therefore, the issue was with my stepdad and his anger, not with me. As a kid, I did not have the self-awareness to understand that. As an adult, I was able to process my memory of the event and see the situation with adult understanding. Just as hoarders hold onto their stuff, a small part of me held onto the belief that I was a bad kid. When I processed this memory as an adult, I understood that I had just been a kid being a kid and I had done nothing wrong.

Sometimes a person's inner self gets stuck in a certain time period. This is because either the time was good—the best in their life—and they want to hold onto it, or there was a break in their spirit, and their spirit is trying to rectify it. I once met a woman who acted like a ten-year-old child. She mentioned that her parents divorced when she was ten. She enjoyed her life when they were together, and a big part of her wanted to remain at that age. She was not ready to adapt to adult circumstances, so she held onto that period of her life when she was happy. I have also met people who enjoyed their life, their family, and all their activities as if they were still in a certain decade, such as the seventies or eighties. Their minds were still in the past, rather than in the current decade, as an attempt to hold onto a time they loved.

Sometimes when a person's mind can't reconcile many upsetting things happening simultaneously, the resulting feelings may turn into looping thoughts, and the person's mind becomes stuck. A specific event also can trigger this. The man whom I found grating because I was jealous of his confidence was similar in some ways to my stepdad. I could not get this man's voice out of my mind for the first few hours after I heard it. I felt like I was seven years old again when I heard him speak. When I processed my feelings about him, I realized the man's voice triggered memories of my stepdad. Analyzing this helped me reconcile traumatic times in my past. Once I understood that the issue with my stepdad was not about me, it was about him, I was able to reconcile feelings from my childhood and let them go.

We once needed beliefs and feelings that later got in the way of living our lives to the fullest. In some cases, they were our protection, our armor, keeping us from being hurt. But there comes a time when we realize that the armor is not keeping us from being hurt; it is keeping us away from other people. The armor becomes what is hurting us. These realizations enable us to put down our fists, open our arms, and trust God, ourselves, and others.

Chapter 6.

CONNECTING AUTHENTICALLY

"We are like islands in the sea, separate on the surface but connected in the deep."

—William James

We are all connected—God, ourselves, and each other. When we hide from ourselves, we hide from each other. When we hide from each other, we hide from ourselves. When we let each other know who we are, we understand we are not so different. And when we find out who we are, we understand our humanness.

I am a person who feels socially awkward at times; I know I am not the only one. I am a person who hopes to live up to my potential but realizes I fall short; I know I am not the only one. I am a person who cherishes the ideals of religion, spiritual practices, and enlightened philosophies; I know I am not the only one. I have found that striving for the ideal is important, but my humanness makes me fall short. I know I am not the only one. Sometimes I say things I wish I did not say and write things I wish I didn't write. I am, at times, awkward, goofy, and perhaps a little weird. I am not the only one. I never stop being amazed at how much humans have in common!

Today, I know myself better than ever because I have come to understand there is no shame in being the way I am. My awkwardness, my goofiness, and my weirdness are who I am, and they make me myself. When I show these traits, I am showing myself. When I see others show their honest traits, even if their behavior does not conform to society, they are showing who they are. If we are reaching for the ideal of growing in the light, it is usually beneficial to show who we are, even if we fall short.

When thinking about myself, others, and life, I often think of the Greek myth about a king named Sisyphus, who was punished by the god Zeus. Zeus forced Sisyphus to roll an immense boulder up a hill for eternity. Seems like an unbearable punishment, but there are those who think that at least Sisyphus always has something to try to attain. He has a goal, purpose, and hope. Though it could be stated that the punishment is creating a hopeless task, to have a goal and a purpose is indeed creating hope.

Perhaps our boulder—our seemingly impossible task—is to live in the light of the spirit and to demonstrate kindness, care, and empathy for others. We may fall short; chances are we will at times. And when we do, we can continue to try. We can always have hope that we will succeed, even if we sometimes fail.

In my practice, I often hear clients bare their souls. I have friends who are genuine with me, showing me who they really are, and I can be genuine with them. I have found that when I am open and vulnerable, I appreciate myself more. When I can admit that I have fallen short, it lessens the pain, and when I can reveal my accomplishments, it magnifies my pride. When we share our pain, our pain is lessened. When we share our joy, our joy is magnified. Sharing honestly with others helps us process our feelings.

I have listened to clients discuss people they have hurt. I have heard friends express sorrow about their behaviors in the past. Over and over in my life, I have heard about harm people have committed against others. But the harm does not make up the entire nature of a person. We are better than our mistakes. When people are open and honest about their regret, I assume they are better than their mistakes. We're often more able to forgive ourselves if we share our mistakes with another person.

For most of us, we have times when everything is good and we don't have much to worry about. Often our most carefree times happen when we are younger. I remember being four years old and not having to worry or be anxious about anything in my life. I was connected to my inner peace, my serenity. Without knowing the words to describe it, I was aware of my inner spirituality. We are all spiritual creatures living in a physical world. We forget that sometimes. Events that happen to us sometimes cause us to forget our spiritual connection. When I allow people to know where I have fallen short, where I have most forgotten my spiritual connection, I am more able to feel the light that is within me and the light that is within others. I need to let go of my darkness to feel my light. When I let go of my darkness and feel my light, I understand more around me.

How do I do that? I tell a trusted person, myself, and God what that darkness is and where I fell short of my ideal. I get rid of that weight so I can better see my inner light. I let go so God can take over. This is an ideal that may not be completely attainable, but making an effort is important. If we make an effort, we can better understand how and why we fall short.

We don't always recognize all the times we have fallen short of the ideal of showing kindness, care, and empathy. Because of my jealousy of John, who was so confident, I did not treat him with the respect I normally show others, and I avoided talking to him. Now that I understand that I was simply jealous of him, I am more respectful. It is unfair for me to treat him less than kindly because of my own issues.

Some people view others as either good or bad, safe or unsafe. I believe there are people who find pleasure in causing harm, truly unsafe people, but I believe those people are rare. In fact, we are more complicated than that. We all have fallen short. We all have not been the type of friend we meant to be. We all have missed an opportunity to help someone in need because we were too busy thinking about ourselves. We all have missed the mark. That does not make us bad people; that makes us human. Religious people do not always show their love, but the ideal encourages us to try. Those who are in twelve-step programs or who strive to live according to other philosophies may fall short, but they have an important ideal they're working toward. We cannot truly know someone by only one action; we learn to know others by their spirit. Our true spirit can feel dimmed by our feelings at times, but this is an illusion. Our spirit is always bright, but we forget due to life and challenging emotions like anger, guilt, and shame. Guilt is our awareness that we did something bad; shame is the belief that we are bad. When we have those feelings, it is often helpful to share them with someone we trust. When we tell others about our feelings, we allow them to show us the grace that God gives us. That is the place where we become truly open and shed our armor.

It does not always feel good to tell people about secrets we have hidden in our hearts, but when we tell a trusted person, it can be worth it. Trusted people are those who do not want to use us or our secrets to help themselves. I have gone to therapy and felt that therapists wanted me to help them, or entertain them, or just agree with them. They lost sight of the reason I was there— to heal. I also have experienced many therapists who were able to meet me where I was and to see, hear, and understand me. I have experienced that unconditional positive support.

Typically, the clients in my practice say they want a better life, to be happier, and to be more connected with their spirituality and their inner selves. This requires giving up emotions that get in the way. We can't get rid of all negative emotions, but we can lessen them. We must retain the capacity for sadness, anger, frustration, and other feelings that may be thought of as negative. We need to acknowledge these feelings but keep them in perspective. When our reaction outweighs the situation, the issue is with us, not the situation. But it helps to understand we have reasons for those feelings and to work through them.

Through the years as a society, we have advised others to pull themselves up by their bootstraps, buck up, and get over it. We want people to not feel bad. If a person is suffering, we want to fix it. When a person dies, some people will tell the mourners that the deceased is in a better place. People do that because they want to help. When a person breaks up with a girlfriend or boyfriend, friends may tell that person they are better off without the relationship. We tell people who are hurting they will be fine and not to worry. We are taught that feelings are wrong. Some people will reference girls and women as being too emotional. Some people say things like, "You are crying like a girl," or "Man up," as if being a woman is wrong. Men are taught to be strong and to not show their feelings or cry. Women are taught not to get angry because it's not ladylike.

Thankfully, I do see this shifting. Younger generations, as a whole, embrace their feelings more, but showing feelings still seems to be an underlying taboo. Honest conversations can help discredit the belief that feelings are bad. When counseling people, I have found it is better to acknowledge clients' feelings with statements like, "I understand you are sad, and it is natural to feel that way." When appropriate, I have also found it can be helpful to say, "What happened to you isn't fair!" We do not always need to make someone feel better by fixing a problem. Sometimes we need to allow people to feel their feelings and know it is okay to do so. It is okay to cry, to get angry, and to feel. It is more than okay; it is good. Acknowledging their feelings can help people be ready to move on.

I had a friend who lost his brother as a result of a car accident. The brother was taken to a hospital, and my friend tried to see him before he passed. There was too much traffic, and my friend did not get there in time. His brother died without seeing his beloved family member, his brother. I cried with him. My friend and I experienced a greater connection by sharing in his vulnerability. It is good to allow ourselves to feel and to share our feelings with others.

Allowing ourselves to feel difficult feelings often lets us move on to comforting feelings. I believe passion is one of the most comforting feelings. When we feel passion about our actions, work, or behaviors, it feels like an intense love. We lose track of time. We are more creative. We are full of joy. Perhaps in some ways, passion is the most intense feeling.

Throughout history, people have made the world a better place because they were passionate about their work. Some of the most influential people have shown their passion, such as Jesus, Dr. Martin Luther King Jr., and Mother Teresa. They had a passion for others and for their work. Michelangelo, Beethoven, and Walt Disney were passionate about their art. Passion changes the world. Feelings change the world.

When I am working with a client, talking with a close friend, or speaking to a congregation, I often feel an intense joy just being around people. I love working with my clients. I'm passionate about helping them. In the past, I was afraid of those feelings. I was afraid it was not appropriate to love people and to feel a passion for people. But now I know such feelings are good; we have them for a reason. When I accepted how I felt, I realized that it is what God wants for me: to love, to care, to empathize, and to be passionate about helping people with my words. God is helping me do what I cannot do alone—find my passion and share it with others. That is why I wrote this book—because I want to share these words.

I hope this book, this chapter, is a catalyst to help you be yourself, to know that being authentically who you are is good, and to not blame yourself for events you had no control over. Instead, share your feelings with another person, mend the past, and exchange darkness for light, anger for passion, and armor for connection.

Chapter 7.

SUPPORTING EACH OTHER

"And the King will answer them, 'Don't you know? When you cared for one of the least of these, my little ones, my true brothers and sisters, you demonstrated love for me.'"

—Matthew 25:40
(The Passion Translation)

Who hasn't been hungry for love and support, only to be left voiceless, like a dream when you are trying to scream and nothing comes out? Who hasn't been in need of emotional comfort and reached out only to find themselves alone? Most of us have been there, and due to our humanness, many of us also have missed opportunities to help others.

Two concepts in scripture related to emotional support stand out to me—that Jesus was full of emotion, and that there are no conditions for receiving God's love. God validates our emotions because God validates us. In life and in my therapy practice, I notice that people often do not like to validate their feelings. More times than I can count, people have told me how they feel and then apologized for it or said they should not feel that way. When we believe we should not feel the way we do, it can cause us to feel even worse.

In our society, we are often made to believe that we should not feel the way we feel. We can begin to question our feelings. Are we taking things too personally? Are we too sensitive? Are we too weak, or just wrong, or unintelligent? If other people say we are "too sensitive," we may want to look at all the sensitive people who have roamed the earth and made great contributions: Shakespeare, Dr. Martin Luther King Jr., Mother Teresa, Frederick Douglass, and Jesus, to name a few.

In John 11:35 (NIV), describing the scene when Jesus encountered those who were mourning the death of Lazarus, it says, "Jesus wept." The following passage doesn't describe others saying Jesus shouldn't cry or asking him why he was crying. Instead, those who were present said, "See how he loved him" (John 11:36, NIV), speaking of Jesus's sorrow for his friend's death.

If we break a bone, people do not say we should not hurt. People do not try to talk us out of feeling the pain. They do not say we should be stronger or ask, "Why are you letting that leg get to you?" Why do people say those things regarding emotions? If we have a feeling, it is our right and privilege to have that feeling. What we do with our feelings could be harmful, but having the feeling is not wrong. If our feelings are out of proportion or overwhelming, it can help to talk with someone about them—a friend, relative, teacher, therapist, or religious affiliate. And by offering support to others when they need it, validating their feelings, and showing we care, we increase our capacity for love and our connection with our Creator.

Throughout time, humans have shown a need for confession. The questions about what we have done, whom we have hurt, and where we were wrong often need answers. Words are powerful, and it is a release when we allow vulnerability by discussing our feelings and shortcomings. It is as if we are saying, "This is the most challenging part of myself. This is the part I don't like. I want you to know that part of me too." When another person is forgiving toward that part of us, that is grace.

And that grace unites us with them and ourselves. We become whole. When we confess to a trusted person, we are fed.

It is difficult to reach out in this way, but we need to do it at times. We do not go on this adventure of life alone. God is with us. People have free will, so we need patience to allow God to provide the right person to talk with, or to be able to talk with the right person at the right time.

I have heard the statement that some people want the best for us and some don't. I don't believe people's motivations are as straightforward as that. In the past, I have been less than a good friend to someone. I have not listened, called, or offered the most caring words when I should have. Other times, I have been there for those people. Sometimes, we miss the mark. We all do. So who is the right person to turn to for help, and how can we be a person who is supportive of others?

The right person is one who responds without judgment and doesn't just remain silent, which feels like abandonment. The right person is one who doesn't compare your actions to his own or make it about him. The right person is one who says, "I wish that didn't happen to you," or "I'm sorry you're hurting." The right person is one who will share her feelings about what happened in your life. The right person is one who cares and shows it. The right person is not stuck in self. The beautiful thing is that life is a journey, not a destination. In this journey, we learn more about ourselves and others when we share our feelings with them and support them when they share their feelings with us.

Chapter 8.

BUILDING A SOLID FOUNDATION OF SELF

"I will not allow my life's light to be determined by the darkness around me."

—Sojourner Truth

My house is typically tidy, but sometimes I notice dust or items out of place that I hadn't noticed previously. When I look under the bed or behind a door, I may see objects that I need to throw away or clean. We can't just clean our houses once and leave it at that. It is an ongoing process. It comes down to knowing what to clean, what to keep, and what to get rid of. It is a journey, not a destination. It can be tempting to throw out too much. It can be tempting to beat ourselves up for having a little dust around. Just as we have cleaning to do in our physical houses, we have cleaning to do in our mental and emotional houses. But the trick is knowing what to clean, when, and how to identify what to clean or throw out. Keeping our house in order is not a one-time event, and neither is maintaining our mental health. We must continue to look at ourselves and determine what we need and what we don't need.

I have formulated steps for better self-awareness that have been helpful to me. Conducting a quick inventory is helpful when I have uncomfortable feelings.

The first step in this inventory process is to understand and name my feelings. I have a friend who is in the music business. He went to the home of a person who had a beautiful music studio. When he thought about how he felt about the studio, he realized he had more than one feeling about it. He was happy for the person who could work with such great equipment, but he also noticed that he felt sad that he didn't have such a studio. He realized he also felt jealousy. He identified the feelings he associated with the studio: happy, sad, and jealous. When he was able to name his feelings, he knew what he was dealing with.

The second step is to understand that it is human to have the feelings we have. When we realize that our feelings are a normal part of being human, a path may appear for further acceptance of the way we feel. My friend, after talking about his jealousy, was able to be happy for his friend because he had such a wonderful studio. He was then able to be grateful for all the things he had. Someone around us will always have less, and someone will always have more. Or as I like to put it in my Tennessee slang, "There is always a bigger dog out there." It is helpful to not compare ourselves to others but instead to be happy for others and happy for what we have.

The third step is to inspect with kindness where the feeling is coming from. My friend used to have a studio and would invite people over to make music. He missed that time and wished for a creative outlet. He was jealous not only of the studio but also of the connection with others through the creative outlet of music.

The fourth step is having compassion for ourselves and the way we're feeling. We can recognize that we have our feelings, but we do not need to allow our feelings to have us. When my friend found compassion for himself, he understood it is human to have the feelings he was having. He also understood that, though his feelings were valid, he appreciated other aspects of his life. He had the ability to rent a music studio to fulfill his creative outlet. He had a wonderful career in the music business and a good life. My friend is basically a happy person, and he understood that he did not need to hold onto the uncomfortable feelings. He could let them go.

Taking such an inventory may seem daunting, but it becomes easier with practice. A way to make it even easier is to adapt it for your own use and make it your own.

A wonderful thing about the quick inventory is that we can not only use it to help ourselves, but we can also use it to help others. If I am talking with someone who has an emotional challenge that is difficult to reconcile, I follow the steps. I ask, "What are you feeling as you talk or think about this?" We can then begin naming the feelings.

Next, I help the person understand that having those feelings is part of being human.

Then I encourage the person to inspect with kindness where the feelings are coming from.

Finally, I help the person accept the feelings with compassion.

This dialogue is easier if we can be vulnerable ourselves. Asking others to look deeper into their feelings is a request to be more vulnerable. It is often easier to encourage someone's vulnerability when we can be vulnerable ourselves.

To get ourselves in a place where we can help others through hardships, we must work on becoming more open and vulnerable … truer to ourselves in order to help others. We have all been given gifts that allow us to be helpful to each other, and when we hide ourselves, we hide those gifts. When we are vulnerable and open about who we are, our gifts come shining through. It is there that we can better understand our foundation of self.

We all have a foundation of self, but life experiences can cause us to forget that foundation. It is up to us and God to determine our foundation. Others may impact our foundation but should not be allowed to create it. The foundation of who we are goes beyond the clothes we wear and how we appear. It is our essence, which can be difficult to put into words. When we do not have a solid foundation, we are at risk of allowing others to dictate who we are. We are giving others the power to dictate our foundation, and we become more vulnerable to what other people think. We could end up helping others just to look good or because we think we should, instead of helping others from a place of genuine compassion. Doing such work without faith is exhausting! Perhaps Oscar Wilde said it best in his book, *The Picture of Dorian Gray*:

"The aim of life is self-development. To realize one's nature perfectly—that is what each of us is here for. People are afraid of themselves, nowadays. They have forgotten the highest of all duties, the duty that one owes to one's self. Of course, they are charitable. They feed the hungry, and clothe the beggar. But their own souls starve, and are naked."

Building a solid foundation takes self-awareness to

determine our own essence and then self-acceptance about what we find.

I am coming to a place in life where I can live more fully because I do not allow others to determine who I am. I can just be who I am. I can live more fully because I can respect others when they admit they are wrong, and I can respect myself when I make amends. My appreciation of myself is often more powerful than others' disapproval. This is a good place to be, and in this place, I can regularly clean away the dust. I can take off the armor with little to no embarrassment and fear. I have built a solid foundation, which allows me to be me and to be available to provide support to others.

I have found this place by naming my feelings, allowing those feelings without guilt, determining where they came from, and letting go of feelings I don't need. Helping others further solidifies who I am. Once we know more about who we are, we are less vulnerable to allowing others to have power over our feelings and thoughts.

CONCLUSION

By identifying and understanding our feelings, finding and following our focal point, getting rid of behaviors that stand in our way, and connecting with others and God, we can find peace, quiet our minds, and live more fully. These processes may be difficult for those who have a psychosis or pathology that must be overcome before they can move forward. But for most people, the strategies I discuss in this book can provide meaningful guidance and a path forward. I use these strategies for myself and in my practice. I have witnessed people moving through their challenging feelings, emerging on the other side, and achieving a quieter mind, more connection with others and God, and a fuller life. May peace be with you as you continue your journey toward living fully!

ACKNOWLEDGMENTS

Thanks to my husband, Kayle Kiener, who helped me carve out time to write this book and believed in my ability to write it.

To my mother, Jo Webster: You were there listening to me with an understanding ear from the beginning, and I finally did it!

I would like to thank Marty Bell for enabling me to speak to the congregation! Thank you for your support!

To the Unitarian Universalist Fellowship of Clarksville in Tennessee, thank you for the love and care and for validating my words. Daniel, I have always loved our conversations!

Michele Nicholson, you are a bright spot in my life! I love talking with you about the concepts behind my writing. Thank you for listening!

Thank you, Ramey Siler. You know how long it took me to finish writing this, and you were impressed that I took on the challenge. Thank you for the respect and confidence you have in me; it has helped inspire this book.

I am grateful to my editor, Jan Stapleman, and my publishing consultant, Richard Wolf. I am honored to know you both, and I thank you for your attention to detail.

And finally, thank you to my friends who shared in my excitement about completing this book.

ABOUT THE AUTHOR

Clancy Kiener is a licensed marriage and family therapist with a master's degree in religion. She enjoys working as a therapist and professional speaker at treatment centers and churches, connecting with people from all walks of life. In her therapy practice, Clancy focuses on empowerment, dreams, connection, and nutrition. She lives in Middle Tennessee with her husband and their temperamental but lovable dog, Joey. Clancy is a proud mom to daughter Sarah. She also enjoys visiting with her mom, who also lives in Tennessee. In her leisure time, Clancy likes to take walks, paint, and write. She has recently taken up writing poetry.

Made in the USA
Columbia, SC
28 August 2023

22103374R00055